BY COMMON SALT

By Common Salt

Killarney Clary

OBERLIN COLLEGE PRESS
FIELD POETRY SERIES

Publication of this book was made possible by a grant from the Lannan Foundation.

Library of Congress Cataloging-in-Publication Data:

Clary, Killarney.
    By Common Salt / Killarney Clary.
    (FIELD Poetry Series; 4)
    I. Title.   II. Series.

LC: 95-071542
ISBN: 0-932440-73-8
    0-932440-74-6 (pbk.)

ACKNOWLEDGMENTS

Grateful acknowledgment is made to the following magazines where some of these poems previously appeared:

American Poetry Review, Arshile, Colorado Review, Epoch, Faultline, Field, L.A. Weekly, Lingo, Missouri Review, Phoebe, Ploughshares, Shiny, South Florida Poetry Review, The Prose Poem, Yale Review.

I would like to thank the people of the Lannan Foundation for their generosity and respect.

For Willene

CONTENTS

I

II

III

Iblis asked, "My God, does there remain a place in which I have not bowed?" God answered, "Yes, the place is on earth. Hurry down there."

Ad-Digarbakri

I

I had a home in the hill with rag-patch-work birds. No blood there, and no women. Worlds hung by their feet as in a water drop. No need to believe or doubt the blue and diamond of the sky weighted and waiting to fall.

Threads instead of feathers caught in the black trees; beggar starlings laughed, ran with heavy strides—not at all like birds—but I didn't know nature's manners or the probable names for the surge of my heart.

So these dervishes drew me through their weave of tunnels and I celebrated. I wouldn't surprise evil in that track, swore never again to wait in fear for a betrayer to rise from my skinned knee. I wasn't innocent. I wanted to be there.

An old woman alone in a white car on Fletcher peers into a pink bakery box as she waits at the signal in twilight. I'm anxious to be home, talking. I'm afraid of the smell of damp metal, a chill that rises into my scalp, a thud against the wall at three a.m.; the phone keeps ringing. When you only have one thing, you're bound to hate it.

Only the size of a hand, a pounded gold boat was disrupted from the bog by the coulter of a plow. Oars no larger than sandwich picks. A mast of bent gold wire.

For two thousand years it sailed an airless voyage, filled and surrounded by black peat. Dark comfort of its secret, the way each part, each piece was suspended and blind. . . .

If there were messages they vibrated and garbled across hammered strap benches; there was no space through which to shout. In perfect sleep. No rocking. No song.

What beauty and what prince, apple or thorn? Was it such trouble to shine empty in daylight? Darker still was that inclination to tip forward and take on heaviness, sigh, "I don't remember." "Don't remember me."

He will come to cause mischief, up from a cavern that holds him like a tone, across asphalt that sparkles in the night. But this is not his road; he crosses this, passes through silver parks.

He will bring me trouble as certain as my body and I will call it all names and have no answer.

He has traveled only straight lines over centuries. Maybe I should move but I don't have anything he'd steal.

He will come when I am cooking and I turn and lift my arm to unlatch the window. I will taste the air then. I will see I'd left no room for it and that I am dying. As I reach for the salt as I step toward the door, as I align myself, call another name, I am still dying.

He would laugh if I chipped that outer corner of the house to free his way or turned the needle's eye to the thread of his whistle. I would sleep well for some time dreaming of one sure thing. If I'm lucky, he will want to win again.

Clear of oak groves, sunrise stretched a thin reach deep into the chamber, tripping the setting of fires on hilltops: signals relayed to the quarters. A day to plant or hunt, enter women or agreements.

Night skies were laid on fields in perfect orientation before the plates opened, wandered, collided; they continue and will. There is so much to take into account. It may be impossible to choose for myself; all pleasures might hand me loneliness.

I'll find the dark room, tip the white table to catch a shaft bent by a mirror, shot through a pin hole, and I'll watch the ocean upside down. Foam churns at the edge of a vision. It is time to do something in particular.

A man with carnations at the stop holds high his index finger, mouths, "one dollar" to each of us with our windows up, air on. Two *Guardian Angels* pass through the traffic, begging money for our safety.

Light beams from police helicopters are slow on the hillside, quick across the lake. They find who they're after, hang above Westerly Terrace as if the shafts could pin him. It works. He is turned to face me, and in the jiggling spot a cop puts one hand on his head and bends him into the car.

North over one of the bridges, everyone was kissing, like they're supposed to in Paris. I'd been alone so long, the picture of my friends lightened in me. If I could only be in the place I was in. So I tried. Now I wonder—which bridge?

Richard cuts back the wisteria; I go to answer the phone. Threads are woven, unwoven in my sleep, tied to the door of the puzzle so I may return.

Makes no difference if I cry or the glass figure shatters. Maybe running out of gasoline is best—somewhere in the desert in Nevada—and I could stand on the roadside in the heat and begin, as I did my first night away, a list of all the people I've ever seen.

In both directions the highway thins to points. Mirages pool on the blacktop like windows to forever, like the borders inside which I am complete, including completely off. Sonora cactus. My blouse. All the stuff in the world too much in my meanders. Before the fourth ring I say hello.

I list in my mind what I have left to do. I don't need to do anything, this close to the heart of my life. Nothing else to buy; I've written a last postcard. "Let me come inside," I plead. Inside what, and who's to answer? What remains is my moving through the cathedral as it moves to me. What's near alters most. Colored light is blocked and let fall by columns and archways with my pace. Mine.

Between surrender and a train ticket, I am interested and alone. I hold coins and then they're spent. I warm my hands at a bank of candles, each lit by someone for something, tall, creamy with their flames reaching together. I want to stay here, for the few hours, on behalf of all I'll never know.

If I can, I'll read birds. Two, let go on opposite coasts, cross in flight, and that marks the place.

Two circles, each drawn through the other's center, describe an almond eye, vessel of the fish. I measure and count, pace to four points, swim the arc that curls always on itself. This is dimension and shape.

But spirit, bottled wisp, blue and red in the glass. I ask like a spire, busy as lodestone and distracted by wanting to be lightning, fuel. If only I could need you.

A lightless place beneath the city, from which emerge wary, puzzled ones who touch the surface of water and recoil.

A pond in a forest. If thin enough, rays through the crown canopy print rounds of sun on the pool floor. Here, hunters reached in but their hands came up empty and the hollow refilled.

The flight of an owl, and what the augur gained he told in the length of his stride.

———————

The advertisement of the skywriter isn't finished and already the opening letter melts to blue. It won't be easy to stop.

At each fold and end I answer; the way won't care. I want to memorize the map but can only hold four moves in mind at once, so I imagine what will come, with hope or fear, depending on the weather.

I am let loose in weather, yet constantly I pray and cater to it. I can't hear my voice above the wind. It is medicine to listen to the wind.

Their boat was lost in the surf. She keened for it; her husband urged her away. They walked together over the storm beach; she didn't hold on to him, but to what he carried: net or rope, his pack of woven straw.

He'd been unable to land the curragh; she was sorry and he, blameless. I can't watch their mix of pardon and disappointment; I turn it off. The world must break.

$\mathbf{A}$ few steps, turns, and the center nears; then the pilgrim's bent away. Toward the finish, so close to the point of entry, despair. Travel seems deliberate enough; pace is the only risk.

A boy who can barely pick out notes flicks open the catches of the case, recklessly lifts the violin, plays the minuet straight through. He would be stunned himself but he's in a hurry.

When the project is finished, energy pines on; its gyro pilot corrects intrusion, re-adjusts its way to its end. It has to end. Another interest glints in a stream.

An aimless game. A good one. There's coffee at the recess, and set-backs go unrecognized. A portion empties, wrings out more.

I've had a number of rosy days, desert-cloud sunrises, windy dusks. I talked with a friend about good stretches, how they end, how they always return. Something is not quite right. A glowing porcelain plate cracks, would bleed a black rush that would vaporize and hang to the foothills. But the break is slow, and I find myself trying to calm it into holding off. "You don't have to do this," I say. "You can be a plate; that's enough."

Now she's blue. I'm fine. It seems the sun is fixed, so it's morning all day. We live in circles and spirals; we walk through grids of new cities, are lost and then go home. Home is the tricky part; things are kept there even when they don't work anymore.

Stretched out, I'm a carrier, open and empty. Storms move quickly in this air. Round, blinking shadows darken anything they pass for an instant, and people change their minds and go away.

Without all the surface that I bet importance upon, I am reception, a clear glass jar without a lid, sinking in Glass Lake. And the fish that trap themselves and struggle inside me are beautiful, foolish and alive. They tire, and when they are without will, the current frees them.

What is the so-much-larger thing, more than the collected waters of the world, more than unhinged light, love and breath? I don't see it in the details now; it is far beyond them. My longing and failure of reason give me hope—an instrument I must learn to play.

You or I, who, by appearances in the air, will be remembered, by walking in a circle might forgive, by common salt will awaken, by the pulsation of some member might have presence, by writings in ashes will trick the future, by wild beasts will begin and end,

We who could divine what is from what is, pull any one way with purpose, win or lose at dice, laugh in the mirror, wish through the tunnels. Risk is juggled into difference.

I have met braves and cowards inside and out, trusted them equally. You or I, who could have been, lost point one day at the very spot where, years later, the accident would happen.

II

Mr. Dooms would meet us across the Bay Bridge at a restaurant that featured "Dancing Waters." Fountains in colored lights. He was a client of my father's; we were to be polite. Later, at his house, his daughters showed us porno pictures in a magazine and then we rode back to our hotel.

I learned about business—that it was a late-night, uneasy entertainment, chilled and full of sparkle. The lights on the bridge and from San Francisco on the dark bay, and the cold car and lack of fun were swept up in exchange for something I would never hear of, because the taboo deals were as delicate as ice in a glass against a glass toasting Friday.

This evening, here in Los Angeles, clerks and managers in their smooth, safe jackets ride the buses home where they turn on lights and TVs. I bend to the sink and as I close my eyes I know now, I am vulnerable now, in the dark of my own hands, in the pleasure of washing.

And in the loneliness of slippers and fear of comfort I breathe, I hold my breath. Tonight's anxiety melts into tomorrow's meeting, a few laughs, a loose thread, a demand flying on the city's own wind.

Doubt howls up from gutter drains to argue with brilliant offices and the determined pace echoes on hard expensive shoes across the parking garage under Pershing Square. I am in between, on edge, patient and gullible while mail is sorted at Terminal Annex and trucks make their way toward Grand Central Market, from Mexico with melons, with flowers from Leucadia.

Even though I lose my secrets repeatedly the unfinished and unseen dance with experience, what cannot be forgotten. Another car is hit head-on. Another friend says, "Don't look."

I set the letter I might send him on the shelf near the atlas outlining countries renamed over the summer which was damper than usual. I wonder if the map makers or weathermen ever wait. I never looked forward to the party; I longed for goodnight, nostalgia and regret, the dishwasher running.

Shopping in Glendale Galleria, if I stand for five minutes a thing happens. A lost child cries but won't talk to me; a few stores away the mother shouts; I show her. In the crowd of rough boys, families, women resembling me, I begin to laugh. I know a kiss would place me and so, in a way, I have it. Centered in a whirl of faces, I am anything but dizzy; sixteen monitors show "Robin Hood." Oh, *that's* who he looks like.

What can anything stand for if to promise is to freeze circumstance? The illusion that growth is a sacred map, the way a member of the meeting will say, "Wrap it up," the ticket line that stretches out—each points to spending life, and the few huge drops of rain dry away in seconds. I am someone else now. Try me again.

I am annoyed as she repeats herself, her excuses for some action that calls for no excuse. She bought the dress. But she wants to explain because of this caused by that, traveling back into a clutter of wrong turns and questions with answers that went on too long.

Some are loved more than others. Some are favored, some bent or cornered. All forms wander and hide, stand wide-winged, wait in readiness or disgrace.

Candles line the stairway, but as if tumbled in a wave I lose my sense of direction. Flickering, this life; and shadows are wavering with a draft, dancing, pulling and drawing, leaning on the untouchable.

Too loud, too bright, too much for me as the party approaches from above and below with stories, moods. I have thought I should learn to arrange what comes to me in this parade or should stand unjudging as it washes about, but I am easily a part of it. My flag. My drum.

Restless before the canary, wave of traffic on an inhale, I can just barely see on a dark blue ground black arabesques. Music begs, "More." Toward Elysian Park the sky pinks, and whispers build into a Santa Ana breeze in the pepper tree. My day opens above the pale rivers of freeways, patterns of tongues and districts; a tapping energy quickens. I am moving.

Light and vibration double and double again. The last cool whirl of dust promises wishes will turn in rage, spin, widen and disappear. I know my hand on the door jamb, hot coffee passing my heart; I believe the stars are still up there.

The attendant at the corner station says, "No wonder my boss likes you; you come for gas three times a day."

The man with the pick-up asks, "What's that you say?" and the attendant laughs and adjusts the folded knife tucked into his belt at his back.

They both laugh.

Last week we bought an ice cream for a sad boy at the Broadway Street Fair. Fluorescent pink toy flamingoes hung by their necks under the awning of the ring-toss booth where a scarred blond man, shaky beneath his interactions, kept an eye on us, an eye on the crowd. It was billed as a fiesta, but days before Cinco de Mayo. To celebrate on a holiday would be crazy.

The high-numbered streets of South-Central, Pico in Koreatown, and Hollywood are on fire. Ratings soar. In the smoky blue quiet of curfew I find the phone lines are jammed, so I watch. Flash of a transformer blowing out, the surrounding blocks go dead, and I can hear young men loud in the dark field by the reservoir; their shouts don't last. A crane fly hisses, crumples like hair on the gas burner.

Maybe they're all singing to themselves, alone in malls, against foot traffic on sidewalks. A small dark boy, kneeling, rubs the chest of a limp man in the parking lot of the 7-Eleven; he's done this before. I can feel the inside of my skin. Don't Walk/Walk. I am a package that moves across the street, enters the frame shop, brushes up against a cockroach that moves away slowly. Hard shells. Long time. My fingernails tap layers of tape on the table while I wait and I think of the calendar to solidify my life in my head. July.

It takes the old man forever to notice me and when he tears the paper backing he cuts himself on the glass. He says he's on blood pressure medication, seems a little frantic. With his finger held high, he turns through a swinging door behind the counter.

The aquatint print of Nancy's photograph that she'd given me as a wedding present fell off the mantle in the earthquake. Three copies of her face-made-spooky, six big ears, dark pools of eyes and mouths.

Thin blood. Speed of light. Black holes. Someone in the back room replaces the glass while the roach wanders around one end of an electrical strip by the rack of oils. When I carry the picture out, it's heavier than before.

I buy bagels. I try to think of everyone I know and will see in the next day who might want bagels and how many and do they like onion.

I'm pulled east from Santa Monica toward the beacon of First Interstate; office lights wipe in rain across the glass as I'm fed downtown. I steer my own surrender north on the Hollywood, off on Silver Lake Boulevard, up the ravine.

Each street's a wrinkle stretched or stained. No hiding. Laugh lines, scars, life lines and futures, places that haven't been kissed for so long. New cuts open and are filled with those who'll take the least pay. Bundles sigh on warehouse docks on Industrial, indelible.

As I undress, the bright crown of the tower holds with its one red warning over the crest, reminds me there is a center. It sees me, too, as I set the alarm. Magnets draw, repel.

Finally stopped, the night suddenly clear, I can sort planes from stars, cats from sirens. Though I know there cannot be a place for restlessness, I collect all I can feel into passion for the city that takes me, moves me, demands I touch it here.

A pretty woman is showing me how to complete a form. She holds it toward me, against her blouse, and points to it as she talks. She looks down at it until her finger is in the right place, then lifts her eyes to me and taps the paper. Clearly, carefully, she has told me, and now I know what to do.

Comes from nowhere, goes nowhere, happens. I hum. You tick. The quake reveals an unnamed fault. I crave the transistor radio's instructions: "Wear shoes." "If you can, draw water." "Eat something." Sitting in the dark stairwell, I hold an apple.

Each person is different, lonely, with a misfiled plan. I'm interested in your description of the absolute enemy; everyone is doing what they think is right. I don't want a gun. All across town car alarms are triggered by the shock. Nothing is stolen.

He's carrying my package to my car for me when he says the mother of a boy who was killed on this corner last night is up the street wailing; he says it's bad and he thought he was through with it; he'd seen it in Vietnam and Beirut. He goes on, listing places all over the world where *it* has been seen by *him*.

You want to defend your property and protect your life. I never asked a stranger for help. I've never been really hungry. I think this is an emergency. Don't shoot.

Certainty presses in, says, "I am power in my mixture, nothing pure, but I encompass all." Presses or needles, pries like light in a chink. I try to stop it. I say I want it. I try to stop it.

Even if I close my eyes I cannot know what I will see. My life is here or here, or knitting into itself, announcing its form and use. I've held the paper sideways so that North is West; I find my keys and try to feel afraid. Nothing I expected ever happened.

The flag flaps, shredded on its halyard above the one-thirty-four as I rush the curve of the on-ramp facing L.A. On a day like this I can see the Pacific from Eagle Rock, and downtown buildings are sharp, reaching up like crystals from the basin.

Since her stroke, I work the crossword with her every Sunday. She calls Saturday and leaves a message on my tape, "This is what's left of your mother."

The red sliver horizon as I leave her in Pasadena is my defense and hope. All of Los Angeles, energy and danger buzzing off power lines, lions in Griffith Park loud at dusk. Out and away, in growing disorder, there is a great deal.

If I pause for an instant this afternoon while wiping the sink board with the yellow sponge to notice the quiet behind the hum, hazy warmth before sitting at the bright table to eat soup, then I want to remember—times after school or home with the flu, hours out of step, when I was a housewife in Redlands running errands alone, something like a yawn, empty and essential. Who's there?

I told her in case she was dying, "I will always be talking to you; you can come to me; I won't be afraid."

When I think of the ones I hate, I see how it goes. I need them to stay put in their bones that can be placed, from which they cannot find me. Stay away, in the world, in time.

As she paused on leaving, a way opened. Worry and approval will not obstruct us. Only sadness, her soft blue-white body at once vanished and beneath my skin, a blessing of her weakness—my left leg tingling before I jostle it awake.

The dog moves out onto the warm bricks; dolls sleep in the weed lot. Here on the edge of the country birds are building their nest in a streetlight.

There is no need to go back. There is no reason that this time should be an old one waiting on the porch in a blanket, that the sky should ask me to take what he remembers about the colors in the trees going off, the yellow light inside a house, or how he lifts the darkness up then lowers his dark self everywhere.

But he asks me to recall what is happening. I know I will lie back as I lie back, I will be caught on the grassland's rim, I cannot excuse myself to him as I am warmed by the earth that gives up its heat for me, for the air, and that I am a line drawn, keeping balance on a thin ridge anywhere, expected within the hour.

She ordered a dress that might work with her bad arm. She's used to being handled now but she doesn't look at me. Something will hurt. Something tears a scab from her face and we'll send the dress back.

I ask if she's discouraged. No. I tell her it isn't a very pretty dress anyway. She's sorry about the trouble. I take the box and leave; I think she feels a failure, but it's me. The fabric is fragile; I try cold water. Maybe no one will notice.

We *are* loved, just don't turn to look too quickly; the center burns flat and vacant. I am certain of a blue sleeve to the side just before it's pulled behind the gate.

Ants are in a panic again, their scouts jittery and fragile. Blasted, powdery days. It's time for him to leave and I think I could've helped but I didn't or maybe I did or help was not the problem or there was no problem or. . . .

Embarrassed to see the predicament and yet to proceed, we proceed. But it's out of anybody's hands—inversion layer, clamps on each hour, constant tugging on the stitch, and pains that rise where they can, leaving the troubled place mute and untended.

A lozenge of rusted light on old carpet, rattle of devil wind. Sycamore leaves big as faces cartwheel across the neighbor's shake roof, because of October; and I am at my parents' house on San Rafael just in case. Metal chimes try to cheer but how can they? Nothing so dispiriting as the weather against itself. That unmelodic glitter is the way those who wait are used. I turn repeatedly and wonder if I hear my mother's bedside bell, my father's voice. Will October play us?

III

In the morning, smoke from the garbage of Soller caught in the blinds. At night, wind from Africa rattled the corrugated plastic in its braces above the terrace, banged the windows open and tossed our maps to the tile. No one else will know.

With each new rooms we learned again to make our breakfasts without blocking each other. Asleep, I'd rest my hand on your waist, or press the arch of my foot against your knee to turn the strange into familiar. Our arguments were fierce and quick; there was nowhere else to go.

Home, we remember differently, and the single force we were breaks. Like all pasts, our travels dress themselves too simply. What we did to each other, unwitnessed, unheard, without advice, feels wild as the desert air, ancient as rain in the fire.

———————

There is a man who, through disease, feels each minute is his first. He says to his wife, "You are the first person I've seen. This is my first cup of coffee." I saw him on television; he was frustrated by his diary that recorded repeatedly, "I have just now woken up."

———————

So quiet, the fog, the urge to pack a suitcase before the sun is up, leave without disturbing anyone. Or would you venture with me into the most treacherous ordinary?

Beyond the flowered sheets that aren't ours, laundered by the mute boy in the yarn-crafter's in town, past the pale blue lace curtains meant to bring brightness, which in the quick daylight throw only a cold and hungry shade, beyond the wind which stretches a long long way—out over the Burren and Atlantic—an ancient prayer rises like instinct.

If there is a way past projects and talk, it runs through my heart as a clear whistle, open and raw. Help me to bear anything more and to strengthen the sere hollow that waits on call. One step further, what breaks?

Tenderness. And a black heart looms behind two faces. The low soul is continuous. But the Evil One is an entire surprise, swallowing surprise. I am mesmerized in the hissing afternoon by the woman next door who brushes her dog in a darkened room. All is not orchestrated to weigh down on me—my mind is sure. But the dew-point rises; the air teems thick and loud. Hair on the crown of my head stands in a chill of sadness. Sadness is its own. Moisture evens differences. Sweat in steam. The dog—that there are two dogs identical in size and shape, and that that is why I feel the day is used up while she grooms the patient silhouette, her right hand pulling firmly, her left smoothing the sheen—doesn't matter. Carelessness is the present he brings me; unkind for me to refuse. How well he knows. I am his. When to let go, his.

He gives me a name, pronounces it clumsily but without question around my tongue so often that it shapes my tongue into his saying it. That seems to be *for* me. Help. Gives me a place as I sink into a curl of sleep where I am pleased to be blind, where I fit against legions of small, sturdy animals furred or slippery and all busy. I wash over them, fill and calm. No wind can loosen, pull at or reshape this silvered membrane, gelled here as a way of belonging. One who looks from above sees a familiar face, thinks all is well.

I have done something I didn't mean to do. I want to run. I want so much to run that I must have done wrong. Blond grass, and inside—a ferret. Swish of the wind. First, two: the field, the clean static royal sky. And then I am in it.

Remorse, pinned at my heels like a shadow, darkens and shelters, melts; it never had much of a shape. I hold my hand, pretending this pale red is red. It's the red I can manage. I am sorry. I say I don't know the reason and the ferret smiles. I am not the least bit.

"Cicadas sizzle in the trees beyond the hum of screens. You promise yourself rain. You say, 'Certainly it will happen; it isn't up to me.' You plead,

'Keep tunneling. Into the granite and powder, into the greasy clay; persist; I will pay you back, I promise.' But you aren't sure you can afford it, and you wish it were true—what you thought as a kid—if you covered your eyes, you'd be invisible.

A bat's shadow flutters, circles the dim square ceiling. You know your mama said she caught fireflies when she was a girl, not too far from here, near Kansas City. She hoped you'd see them. You want, tonight, to see them.

Sure. You think anything can get past me?"

I cushion with the pads of my fingertips the corners of a square mirror. Let me twist the sunlight until it blinds you with cheer.

I tell you what I look forward to: stopping in Arizona, who will meet me there. I've wanted to go for years but can't say why, and you are silent waiting for the story of what I leave.

A faint current tickles my sore. If I laugh you'll call me a liar. But I know when I look up at the TV I'll see yet another cheetah gnawing at the soft parts of a gazelle. Surprised prey and the voice-over explaining the order of nature are so like the newest plans for a well life.

Let me say I'm fine. There is no withholding, no gift or theft, just poisons breaking into sugar.

"You might tether possibilities, take into account rays of light which fan from the ocean floor, or tie down the path of surface shimmer that follows you no matter what direction; by considering the outer region of the big bang where beginning has not yet visited, might place yourself in wandering."

A plumb becomes a pendulum. Orbit's a kind of center, I guess. There need not be fractures in thinking. He says there is perfection, no argument, hair braided each morning and a fresh ribbon the color of the dress.

Phone poles snap by as I pass. Their shadows angle around the car in a pattern I would fit to my pulse, match to the turn blinker. Out of phase, but no one else has noticed, and there is a way to save the system. He says if I am diligently clever I will succeed.

"Own one cup, one plate. Change address frequently; never tell your mother's maiden name. Like all nomads you will grow in expertise of geometry and rhythm. On this quest toward the abstract, seamless One, I escort you."

Tools for squaring the circle. Resolution of graph paper. The clocks that push and pull dishevelment. I've tried. Couldn't I be wilier? Couldn't I make a mistake?

"Take my hand. Come down the steps into this little room where it is dark and warm. You don't have to live."

Where light falls between the door and frame onto the polished floor, where I put my hand at dusk in the grass while birds tune their orchestra, louder, more players until the air is all sound. . . .

If I don't have time, I feel the shadow swelling and desperation in song. Come to me where I am. I am not enough.

An unlikely one will guide me; I won't know I'm being helped. Will I know I am in trouble, that there's a distance to be crossed?

A fair life wouldn't tidy itself so well before its end.

I watch for the crone in the wood, helpful toad, cup of blood, distracted from peripheral magic. In my hasty desire I send away the boat that might carry me over.

But it's justice that the trickster slips every one of us a joke, the thing we live and die for. Serves us right and serves us well. Who watches? Heroes are busy. Teachers are busy. Purpose is silent as ever, patient in folds of time.

If I came to the edge of my own, past streams of smoke and the noise of turbulence, handed-off delusion and want, then I could let go of my precious heartache.

Burning ears, palms that itch, a brief flash beyond the hills. What I've learned has been added to me—superstition as sure as numbers.

In the thick of uneasiness, a bit of the unreal peels away, leaves a new and pretty wound through to a ruffled spirit.

A future spins out of dust. Star of milk-weed from the windy spiral shivers in the rough corner. What spider's web or peeled paint, what desire to lie among loose petals and broken hair, what lazy need holds to dreams of a love that is all me?

I wonder on cold nights when we are shut in, asleep, as I breathe your breath, how long it would take until all air was ours. For this, it is essential that your skin leaves mine, and that my own leaves me too, unsuccored.

A smooth, pretty stone for a long time. Damp hands. Ocean push and rattle. In my palm, coarse sand— a new number amid useful trees of rest. Each comes alone to these amazements: time, heart's location, talk or common animals, carries alone the confusion of what is wrong; it can only be carried.

Hibiscus drop through their leaves in the dark; you are asleep. Tin box, wooden shoe, plastic bird—spaced evenly in the heat on the sill. The orchard is haunted, talks through its colors in a known light, and the clouds come in rows to carry the moon over a century plant at the hill crest. "Are you asleep?" I ask from dark trees. Alone, I slip through a secret way; I hear water where I blindly gather almonds for later.

Trinkets rain through the rubber tree; the yard is full. I want to tell you now why I think of the sea, broken things and what won't be still: my hand there, out on the rise and fall. Take this home for me if you are going, this curve of worn glass I found in the lemon grove.

Tight and tense as a swarm of gnats hanging above the humid field, busy and separate as that—the nerves of the day and tick in my veins. I am home, but the work phone rings on; my fingertips spell out what I think; my thumb falls to a space-bar miles away now.

Calm begins as another annoyance, disruption in the gathering hum, a gummy substance clogging the machinery that runs endless conversations in my mind. But then the grasses bend together, uncover music in their silver variations. A singular, deeper note rises above the green and holds and builds as it pulls all else toward it. The last leaf on the sycamore shivers. The dance of shadows inside flutters uneasily, melts beneath an early cloud, begins again.

Two large birds come to rest in the reservoir, gently upsetting the surface, odd mixture of purpose and hesitation. Beyond them, an alien, forbidden forest, mysterious calls for territory or sustenance, calls and answers, swift steps and the heavy whisper of wings weighted by prey. Pale bulbs awaken in rich black slip. Caressed by faceless creatures of damp tangle, they set themselves a direction and press out of their hearts into chance.

Where meadows meet the beach, dunes hush their skin easily in one place or another. Secrets are sifted through velvet shades in bends and hollows.

It is the tide that demands, the waves that begin to beg. With one huge body, the ocean drums, and against it the dark sky lowers, fills with its power caves where petty, sorry animals dream of disappearing, of no longer knowing their own cries.

Below the goodness of night and open laughter of stars, the mighty storm shudders, flashes, passes quickly before a tender lull, and a great red silence.

They prepare with Sherpa porters in the foothills beneath a sharp white peak still lit. Packing in cold shadows where cold is a solid, weighing and settling routes, distracted by delicate anxious campfires, they find it difficult to lift their eyes. A footstep's a rift, every premonition a glacier. About this material there is no question.

Of a heavy butterfly, disproportionately large, gray in a gray magnolia tree beyond a room-sized, cloudy, plate glass window. Thick, burdened flapping in the leathery leaves.

Of a woman who came toward me in the dark and showed me her body and was hurt when I refused to play. When I pitied her, her face turned into a Balinese mask all teeth and evil. My body.

Of watching from the oceanfront a fire on an island where cancer was being made in the basement. Foam on the waves black with ash.

Of a tidal marsh in the moonlight, of flying inches above silver water and silt bars, through the stillness among great blue herons and snowy egrets wise but cruel.

Of sinking in skin in a closed place. Of all parts laid out in order and ready.

The wild boy of Aveyron who drinks his cool water from a cup, cries an unnamable weight. The water may be sweet but it stands for something to him now; he doesn't taste this drink. And I may not love any thing or one, but I might love, as once he swallowed before he was apart.

They'll keep me from hurting myself. Let enter what enters—energy in a bead of the hundred beads of a necklace. Spin. His ringed fingers cool on my forehead, his bells watchful, he is nourished by a face that closes and begs; I, by a spirit loosening my crazy arms and pounding step. He holds me; I hold tight my fists. No object suffices.

Back in the solid world, alone at night, I remove bracelets and scarves, unwind the cloth from my body like the dressing from a wound. Hungry for potatoes then, thirsty for water. Twirl and rattle, glitter and sway. I call from a vacant lot, "Food." "Food."

Water echoes under the bridge, dark slap against the pilings. A drop in the cistern rings. Stars clot and spread atop a black membrane, shuttle into swells, smear against the wales of the rowboat. Kiss.

"If you are this happy you will soon die."

I cup the sparkling bay in my hand, let it leak through.
No I will not.

ABOUT THE AUTHOR

*Killarney Clary is the author of
a previous collection of poetry,*
Who Whispered Near Me, *and a
chapbook,* By Me, By Any, Can
and Can't Be Done. *She is the
recipient of a fellowship from
the Lannan Foundation. She
lives in Los Angeles.*

COLOPHON

*Designed by Steve Farkas
Composition by Professional Book Compositors
in 11 point Garamond Book typeface
Printed by Cushing-Malloy
on 60# Glatfelter*